HIDDEN IN
PLAIN SIGHT

WITH ART BY CAROL AYMAR ARMSTRONG

HIDDEN IN PLAIN SIGHT

The Practice of Christian Meditation

AVERY BROOKE

The Upper Room

Nashville, Tennessee

Hidden in Plain Sight

Upper Room edition published in 1986.

Originally published by Seabury Press in 1978.

Scripture quotations not otherwise designated are from the King James Version of the Bible.

Scripture quotations designated RSV are from the Revised Standard Version of the Bible, copyrighted 1946, 1952, and © 1971 by the Division of Christian Education, National Council of Churches of Christ in the United States of America, and are used by permission.

Excerpt from *Psalms for the Common Reader* by Mary Ellen Chase is used by permission of W. W. Norton and Company.

Excerpt from *The Story of Civilization* by Will Durant used by permission of Simon and Schuster.

Excerpt from *Christian Worship, Its Origins and Evolution* by Louis Duschesne used by permission of S.P.C.K., Holy Trinity Church, London, England.

Excerpt from *Bread in the Wilderness* by Thomas Merton, copyright © 1953 by Our Lady of Gethsemane Monastery. Reprinted by permission of New Directions Publishing Corporation.

Excerpt adaped from "Litany for the Nation (Year C);" THE WORSHIPBOOK—SERVICES AND HYMNS. Copyright © MCMLXX The Westminster Press. Adapted and used by permission.

Excerpt from *The Way of a Pilgrim*, trans. by R. M. French used by permission of Harper and Row Publishers, Inc. and S.P.C.K., Holy Trinity Church, London England.

Albert Edward Bailey, excerpted from *The Gospel In Hymns: Backgrounds And Interpretations*. Copyright 1950 Charles Scribner's Sons; copyright renewed © 1978. Reprinted with the permission of Charles Scribner's Sons.

Library of Congress
Cataloging in Publication Data
Brooke, Avery
Hidden in plain sight
"A Vineyard book."

1. Meditation.   I. Title.
BV4813.B68   248'.3   77-17548

First Upper Room Printing: October, 1986 (5)
ISBN 0-8358-0547-6

Printed in the United States of America

CONTENTS

PROLOGUE

Prior to the influx of meditative practices from Hinduism and Buddhism, probably the most common use of the word *meditation* in the West was on signs in front of churches proclaiming: THIS CHURCH IS OPEN FOR PRAYER AND MEDITATION. In monasteries and convents and among a few lay people, both Catholic and Protestant, the very specific and complex methods of meditation developed by St. Ignatius and others were known and used, but such knowledge was an exception. Here and there groups and individuals practiced zen, yoga, or other non-Christian forms of meditation, but they too were exceptions.

We were not only vague about what meditation meant, most of us were disinterested. In the first half of the twentieth century, people weren't particularly interested in prayer either. A spiritual vacuum had arisen within Christianity. When meditative practices, stemming primarily from Hinduism and Buddhism, began to be readily available, those who were spiritually hungry turned to them with eagerness.

In response to this phenomenon a number of Christians have written books and articles. A few of these have denounced non-Christian forms of meditation, but the majority have attempted to explain or adapt them for Christian use. With few exceptions, what has been ignored is Christianity's own vast heritage of meditative practice. One reason for this is that a great deal of Christian meditation is unrecognized as meditation. It is called by other names, forgotten by history, or known to one denomination but not to others.

Sometimes treasures are hidden in plain sight, and when found, they are recognized to be of great worth. It is my purpose in this book to point out a few such treasures of Christian meditation and hold them up to the light so that they will not only be recognized, but be honored and used. I believe that we can and should learn from non-Christian forms of meditation, but that is no reason for Christians to ignore their own inheritance.

I

NATURAL MEDITATION
AND
CHRISTIAN PRAYER

Meditation means many different things to many different people but sometimes we cannot see the forest for the trees and no single tree is the whole forest. Therefore, before considering Christian meditation in particular, it seems wise to take a look at meditation in general.

The word *meditation* is used to describe a state of mind that is at one and the same time both unusually relaxed and unusually aware. This state of mind may either arise naturally or by a great variety of methods, both spiritual and secular. These methods are also called meditation. However a meditative state of mind is achieved, it not only brings relaxation and awareness, but opens doors to new thoughts and feelings welling up from the deeper reaches of the mind.

This definition is broad in scope and based on the natural processes of the human mind and heart rather than on the theological concept of any one religion. In other words, we all meditate, but some of us meditate a great deal and others hardly ever.

It is useful to go back in our imaginations to more primitive times and think of shepherds. It was when Moses was tending the flock of his father-in-law, Jethro, that God called to him out of the burning bush to ask him to do the unlikely, the impossible, and rescue the children of Israel from Egypt. The character of King David was formed while tending his father's flocks. St. Patrick's first trip to Ireland was as a slave where he tended sheep for seven years before he heard God telling him to escape, and later to come back and convert his captors.

I do not mean to imply that a high proportion of shepherds become prophets or saints, or even that they are apt to be religious. My point is that watching sheep is an occupation that is not so completely absorbing that it keeps you from looking out over the fields and meditating. One part of your mind is geared to sheep. The deeper reaches of your mind are free.

Our lives are far from pastoral today. Our sheep and cows and pigs and horses are fenced in. And that is just a beginning. Hundreds—thousands—of timesavers give us time to do other things, but lose us that *meditative* time we used to have while working on simple tasks.

Jesus was a carpenter. With a great deal of hand carpentry there is some space left in your mind for meditative daydreaming—prayerful or otherwise. But if you daydream with today's power saws, you lose a few fingertips. The lumber probably came to the carpenter's shop by camel or donkey with a man or boy walking along beside. Our lumber comes in trucks and trains. You *can* meditate a bit while driving, but not as well as when walking beside a donkey. Jesus' mother walked to the well for water, washing the clothes by hand, and swept the floor with a broom. It was not an easy way of life, but there was time to ponder words in her heart.

There is an unexpected resemblance between these natural ways of meditation, those methods that are described as "purely secular," and the methods taught and practiced today by practictioners of the many traditional or derivative forms of Hindu, Buddhist, and Islamic meditation that have become available and popular in the West. The resemblance is this: To meditate you need interior space. Mind space. This doesn't mean time when you are doing nothing at all, but time when what you are doing is simple enough to occupy only the foreground of your mind.

I am not saying that to meditate one *has* to concentrate on a simple activity at the same time, but the evidence of a broad spectrum of teachers is overwhelming: When you wish to learn how to meditate—rather than just having it come naturally—you are advised to concentrate on something simple in the foreground of your mind. You can say one-two, one-two, one-two—a thousand times or more. You can repeat a nonsense syllable, a phrase packed with meaning, or the word *God* over and over and over. You can concentrate on breathing or on sitting still. You can repeat longer prayers you know by heart and count them on a string of beads. All of these activities are like watching sheep or walking to the well for water in that they occupy the foreground of the mind and leave the deeper reaches open.

Another aspect of human experience that is related to meditation is the widespread interest in crafts and other spare time occupations such as gardening, cooking, bicycling, jogging, and cross-country skiing that hark back to older, simpler ways. Do we engage in these activities only for reasons of fun, or health, nostalgia, or money saving? These are certainly reasons enough, yet perhaps we are also unconsciously seeking time to find that image of God that is within us.

There is, of course, nothing necessarily religious about natural meditation. One may philosophize and daydream and let the mind wander as it will without a single thought about God. For meditation to become religious, a certain attitude must be added. I have sympathy for the position of those who argue that meditation is not religious. Its *origins* are religious, the mantras may be religious, the person meditating may be religious, but if someone brings a secular attitude to the practice of meditation, then it isn't particularly religious. Certainly watching sheep, jogging, washing dishes in the sink, and making clay pots are not religious occupations of themselves.

THE
KINGDOM OF GOD
IS, WITHIN, YOU

How may we use these secular activities that are naturally meditative for Christian meditation? We may bless them. To bless means to consecrate something to God. The most ordinary secular activity may thus become an opportunity for something far more meaningful. There is a lovely old verb used by Celtic Christians: *to sain*. To sain means to bless with the sign of the cross. The Celtic Christians sained practically everything. Even old Druidic customs which didn't directly conflict with Christian beliefs were just sort of baptized, or sained, into the Christian faith. The Celts had blessings and invocations for waking in the morning, kindling the fire, and eating breakfast. They had them for milking the cows, for each cow and calf, each sheep and lamb. There were invocations for fishing and fish, planting and plants, for harvesting, resting, sleeping, dying. The living of their lives and their sense of God's presence were seldom separated.

If we are unable to live such God-conscious lives, we can at least bless a few of our simplest activities. Such a dedication can be totally informal, even wordless, or a traditional blessing or prayer that suits your personality and task. By so dedicating the task, the time, and our thoughts during that time to God, we may turn natural meditation into spiritual meditation.

COMMIT
THY WORKS
UNTO THE LORD

AND THY THOUGHTS
SHALL BE
ESTABLISHED

When people write about meditative experiences, they condense them. All the time that Moses *didn't* hear God speaking from the burning bush doesn't get recorded. Besides, condensed or not, the written word is of a different nature than those thoughts that come and go in the freedom of our minds. Such an interlacing and interlocking of ideas pass and repass before us. When we force them into channels—as we have to do a great deal of the time—that is another matter, for meditation is not channeled, but free.

A Christian blessing—or whatever attitude we bring to our meditation—gives our thoughts a starting place, no more. After that, by the association of ideas, our minds drift from one thought to another. Sometimes several ideas seem to flit through the mind at once or in quick succession. Each human being is a storehouse of feelings, moods, facts, images, stories, incidents, concepts, desires, whole fields of knowledge, and scraps of information much vaster than the storage capabilities of the largest computer in existence. But the biggest difference between our minds and computers is that computers are channeled—programmed—and our minds may either think in channels or run free, as we wish.

Without the opportunities for natural meditation that life provided in simpler times, we must search for them and save them as quiet, sanctified islands of time, set apart from rush and tension. The greatest example we have of sanctified time is the Sabbath. Christians today generally—or partially—forget the commandment: "To remember the Sabbath day, to keep it holy." Our attitude towards Sunday has become similar to our attitude towards the other six days. We may physically stop working, but our minds continue to spin in a turmoil of fragmented thought. Often the day is no more blessed, no more restful, no more whole or holy than the rest of the week.

It is useful to remember that the Sabbath is not just a day, it is a concept, a principle, and a commandment. Sabbath time is sanctified time. It is the spirit of Sabbath that is at the heart of the matter. And keeping it. Not when, or exactly how. Jesus sometimes broke the Sabbath, but he also sometimes escaped the crowds—escaped those who *needed* him—and went off alone to pray. As Jesus said, "The Sabbath was made for man, not man for the Sabbath."

I have a friend, a minister, who has made a deep study of Judaism. He keeps the Sabbath on Saturday as the Jews do. For a minister, Sunday may be a day of worship, but it is also a day of work. On Saturday my friend keeps his Sabbath in his own way. His general rule is to do nothing that he considers work. If he enjoys writing a letter, he does. If he enjoys caring for the garden, he does. He and his wife also start the Sabbath on Friday night with the traditional Jewish blessing.

My friend has a whole day to keep Sabbath, but it need not be a day. One may keep a few moments in the spirit of the Sabbath. It is not enough, but it is a start. For most people Sunday is probably still the best day to rest and remember in sanctified time, even if we may not save the whole day. Church starts us off, and we and the day are blessed. Then ahead of us lie many possibilities. If my friend can garden on his Sabbath, what can we do? I swing now full circle to those quiet activities that free the mind for meditation. It all depends, of course, on how we approach them. If raking the lawn is a cursed chore, then it is not material for the Sabbath. But if it is a glorious day, you need some exercise, and you look at the job with delight and joy in God's creation, then it is right for the Sabbath. Once it is work, drop the rake.

If we are open to God in quiet and sanctified time, if we let *God* write the agenda and initiate the subject of conversation, what might that subject be? What might God say? It is a frightening thought. It takes a great deal more faith and courage to be open to what God may say than it does to speak to God. Yet God also knows our lack of faith, our lack of courage, our lack of strength. We may like what God says or we may not, but he will not ask of us more than we are able.

Part of the reason for our lack of faith and courage is that we both fear and desire a clear, strong message from God. Yet God seldom speaks through a burning bush. God speaks in whispers. Whispers flashing through our minds as we meditate. Whispers in words or wordless. Whispers coming to us seemingly from nowhere when our minds are not too busy to hear. Whispers resulting from some happening in the day, from a few words we read or hear.

But to hear whispers takes listening. To a large extent, all religious meditation, and certainly all Christian meditation, is listening prayer. Whatever the method, the purpose is to listen. But listening doesn't mean straining to hear, it means stilling the turmoil of our minds so that we *may* hear.

Listening to God is prayer, but most of our prayer is apt to be either asking God something or telling God something rather than listening: "God, my life is a mess, help me"; "My child is in trouble, where shall I turn?"; "My marriage is coming apart, what shall I do?"; "God, help my boss to understand me"; "Christ, help me to find a job." Or our words may be expressions of love, of confession, or of thanksgiving. If that is all, something is missing. Prayer should be, is, a two-way street. Prayer, to be complete, must be some sort of communication with, or being with, God and not just our own words to God.

Hinduism and Buddhism tend to use the word *meditation* to mean both more and less than listening to God. Their aim in meditation is often described as a great stillness, a great emptiness. This is far from unknown in Christianity, but is usually called contemplative prayer (a wordless, imageless looking at or being with God). Christian writings on contemplative prayer are apt to be by, or about, those who are considered mystics and often these mystics are also great saints. We all have a touch of the mystic about us and even a touch of saintliness, but few of us are full-time mystics.

The highest form of contemplative prayer (which is mysticism at its best) is a gift from God. St. Teresa of Avila said:

> The highest and most perfect prayer is contemplation. But this is altogether the work of God, as it is supernatural and above our powers. The soul can only prepare itself for this prayer and is able to do nothing in it.

Yet, even a purely secular form of meditation does help to prepare the way, and sometimes in the peace of meditation any of us may experience a touch of what it means to have God take over the work of prayer. The beginner in the spiritual life often knows something of the heights, and the saint becomes simple again.

My favorite theological word is *emphasis*. All facets of all religions appear to a greater or lesser extent in all other religions, but the emphasis often varies tremendously. It is important to a clear understanding of meditation to recognize one major difference in emphasis between Hindu-Buddhist and Christian meditation. This difference is that Christian meditation, as opposed to Hindu-Buddhist meditation, emphasizes God's *immanence*.

Words again! *Immanent* is an awkward word because it sounds like *imminent* (about to happen) or *eminent* (distinguished). Immanent is the opposite of transcendent and means God's presence within us and all the world. Transcendent means God beyond us. Christ came to the world that his Father made. He redeemed that world and sent the Spirit as a light to guide and comfort us.

It is possible to find quotations from Christian mystics that tell you to put all earthly things out of your mind, but you find few of them. How could it be otherwise when we espouse a religion that centers upon God coming into the world as a human being?

The stillness of Christian meditation may sometimes be as still as contemplation. But however still, however seemingly empty those inner reaches of our minds become, Christ is there—and with Christ all creation. In the Christian life, God and the world are both very real and inextricably entangled.

GOD IS
WITH US

I have said that Christian meditation is the listening half of prayer. This means that *all* Christian prayer has the potential of being part meditation. This includes those prayers we say to God in our own words. How may our pleas for help, our words of confession, thanksgiving, and love become more than a monologue? As with turning natural meditation into Christian meditation, the answer lies partly in what attitude we start with. Here it is not a simple matter of blessing a task and then letting the mind wander, for we have already set the mind on its course. The change comes when we trust God enough to allow him to turn the course of our thoughts.

Sometimes God's reply comes to us through our words to him. We begin with our own version and continue the inner monologue, and yet the monologue subtly shifts from our version to God's version. We see the subject in another light, or a fresh possibility comes to mind. With some people, prayer in their own words is more clearly a dialogue with God. I do not mean anything dramatic by this, but simply listening to God through an inner conversation.

Probably even more often God does not answer in words at all, but in an inner sense, feeling, or image. Suddenly we know that it will be all right, or we are overcome by a feeling of peace or forgiveness, or our hearts are turned from bitterness to acceptance, from despair to hope. We see a problem in a new light, inner doors open to new paths. How does this differ from contemplation? As I have said, sometimes Christian meditation *becomes* contemplation, but Christian contemplation, whether it is mystical and "altogether the work of God" or a simple willed looking at or being with God, is quieter. In Christian contemplation, we do not try to have a dialogue with God, it is a matter of silent companionship.

II

CHRISTIAN
MANTRAS

There is no English equivalent for the Hindu word *mantra,* but there are Christian mantras and Christians use them. In classical Hinduism a mantra is either the word *OM* or *AUM*—meaning God—or it is a word, verse, or sentence that reveals God. A mantra is often used for meditation by repeating it over and over. Christian mantras may be defined in exactly the same way. That is, they are either the word *God* or words for God such as Jesus, Lord, or Lord Jesus Christ, or they are short central statements that imply God. (One difference remains: To Hindus the *sound* of a mantra has great significance while to Christians this is usually considered less important.)

Since the time of the early Church, Christians have preached, baptized, and healed the sick "in His name." Yet we also call Jesus by many names: the Christ, the Word made flesh, Lamb of God, King, Lord, Savior, Shepherd. The name of Jesus is, of course, not just a word but all that is implied by that word. Similarly, any mantra, whether a name of God or a few words pointing to him, implies all that God means.

Repeating the name of Jesus a number of times, either within a short prayer or alone, has been natural to Christians since our Lord walked this earth. It is something that just comes to one:—"Jesus, Jesus, Jesus . . ." By the sixth century this spontaneous prayer had developed into a method using the prayer: "Lord Jesus Christ, have mercy on me." Familiarly known as the *Jesus prayer,* this prayer—or slight variations of it—has always had a central place in the spirituality of the Eastern Orthodox Church. Over the centuries, whole systems of teaching have developed about the Jesus prayer. These include tying the repetition of the words to your breathing or to the beat of your heart. In the West, it has become better known because of a remarkable book *The Way of a Pilgrim.* Written in nineteenth-century Russia by an anonymous Christian, it begins as follows:

> By the grace of God I am a Christian man, by my actions a great sinner, and by calling a homeless wanderer of the humblest birth who roams from place to place. My worldly goods are a knapsack with some dried bread in it on my back, and in my breast-pocket a Bible. And that is all.

> On the 24th Sunday after Pentecost I went to church to say my prayers there during the Liturgy. The first Epistle of St. Paul to the Thessalonians was being read, and among other words I heard these—*"Pray without ceasing."* It was this text, more than any other, which forced itself upon my mind, and I began to think how it was possible to pray without ceasing, since a man has to concern himself with other things also in order to make a living . . . I thought and thought, but knew not what to make of it. "What ought I to do?" I thought. "Where shall I find someone to explain it to me?"

LORD JESUS CHRIST
HAVE MERCY ON ME

This practice of repeating a name of God, a short prayer, verse, or phrase has never been restricted to the Orthodox Churches, although there it became and has remained an art and a method, while with most Christians the practice comes from the heart and without plan. A story of St. Francis of Assisi illustrates this:

For over two years Bernard da Quintavalle, one of the most highly respected citizens of Assisi, had been watching Francis's activities. He had seen the roistering young son of a wealthy cloth merchant suddenly and surprisingly leave his father's house and become a shabby beggar, making it his work to repair neglected chapels and churches, to pray, to minister to the poor, and to preach in the streets of Assisi. He found himself greatly moved by the obvious sincerity of young Francis, and by his steadfastness and serenity in the face of the jeers of his former companions.

Eventually Bernard invited Francis to his house. The two talked long and earnestly, and Bernard asked him to spend the night. Choosing to stay in the same room, Bernard feigned sleep, but actually he was watching Francis through half-closed eyes. After some time had passed, he observed Francis rise and kneel and for a long time softly repeat the words: "My God and my all. My God and my all. My God and my all."

Bernard heard and in the morning became the first of the more than five thousand companions and disciples who were to join Francis within the next ten years.

MY GOD
AND MY ALL
MY GOD AND
MY ALL MY GOD
AND MY ALL
MY GOD AND
MY ALL

Mantras must be capable of easy repetition. Words and phrases, however beautiful, that make you stutter and stumble in your mind when used in repetition are not useful as mantras. For this reason, short mantras are usually best.

Glory to God

Thou

Even so, come Lord Jesus.

The joy of the Lord is your strength.

Thy kingdom come, thy will be done.

Let every creature have your love.

O Lord, My God and my Redeemer

Teach me what I do not see.

We are the temple of the living God.

Lord Jesus Christ

Love one another as I have loved you.

Lose your life to find it.

Prepare the way of the Lord.

Hallowed by thy name.

Behold the Lamb of God.

If any one thirst, let him come to me.

Once I was blind and now I see.

 LOVE

ONE  ANOTHER

AS I HAVE

LOVED YOU

Sometimes longer mantras seem better, such as the following:

Worship the Lord in the beauty of holiness.
Let the whole earth stand in awe of him.

Seek and you shall find; knock and it shall open.

Bless the Lord, O my soul.
All that is within me,
bless his holy name

Thou art the Christ, Son of the living God.

Thine is the kingdom,
and the power and the glory,
for ever and ever. Amen.

Create in me a clean heart, O God;
and renew a right spirit within me.

Except a man be born again he cannot see the kingdom of God.

Holy, holy, holy, Lord God Almighty,
which was, and is, and is to come.

You shall know the truth and the truth shall make you free.

Lift up your heads, O ye gates.
Lift them up ye everlasting doors,
and the King of glory shall come in.

Lo, I am with you always, even to the end of time.

IN HIM

WE LIVE AND MOVE

AND HAVE OUR BEING

I said earlier that a mantra is either a name for God or implies God, but if you look over the lists just given, you will see that mantras often include some aspect of our *relationship* with God. This can also be true in other religions, and it helps us to gain perspective to pause and consider how other faiths use a mantra.

A beautiful Jewish example is given by Rabbi Mel Gottlieb: "A few years ago, I was sitting in Jerusalem, in the Novardock yeshiva on the *Shabbat* between *Rosh Hashanah* and *Yom Kippur,* listening to a great musarnik, Rabbi Ben Tzion Brook. It darkened, evening came, and Rabbi Brook kept repeating one verse in singsong fashion from the Song of Songs (2:16):

> My beloved is mine and I am my beloved's, who feeds among the lilies. My beloved is mine, and I am my beloved's, who feeds among the lilies . . . God only wants a little bit of the lilies, a little bit of the heart of man. He doesn't want your automobiles. He doesn't want your coolness, your selfcontrol, your closedness. He wants an open heart, a little bit of the lilies from each man.

This singsong went on and on. He spoke to each man, to each heart, and after a while the bearded Jerusalemites sitting next to me began to beat their hearts. Tears began to flow. The fear, the control, the mistrust was shattered, and their full hearts were open."

AN OPEN HEART

Moslems repeat Dhikers much as Christians may repeat the Jesus prayer. The word *Dhiker* may be translated as remembrance or recollection, *Dhiker Allah* meaning recollection of God. The Koran teaches that there is no greater worship than to be remembering God at all times, and Dhikers are employed to help remember him. Popular Dhikers are *la ilaha illa 'llah* (There is no God but God) or a series of *subhan' Allah* (Glory to God), *al-hamdililah* (Thanks be to God), and *Allahu akbar* (Only God is Great). I include the Arabic words because in spite of the strangeness of Arabic to our ears, we can see how the beauty of the sounds is an aid to repetition.

Whether in Arabic or English, each one of those Moslem Dhikers could be used as a Christian mantra; indeed *Thanks be to God* and *Glory to God* are familiar words to all Christians.

The choice of a mantra is a very personal matter. Even though they all point to God, some words and phrases are more meaningful, or feel more comfortable, to one person than another. Often the best ones are those that spring to mind from your own imagination or your memory of some words from a prayer or the Bible. You need not have one mantra for life—although if your heart so chooses, you may. All mantras point to God, but from different vantage points. As we change and grow, new vistas—or the need for them—may cry out inside us and should not be denied. I even find that sometimes when I am repeating a mantra it will just quietly change, and suddenly I realize that I am repeating a different one. Yet, for another person one mantra will reflect the infinite riches of God for a lifetime.

GLORY
TO GOD

III

MEANING BEYOND
MEANINGS

The Use of
Christian Mantras

How does one use a mantra? There are many ways, but the basic method is incredibly simple: Pick a quiet place and a time of day when you are not apt to be interrupted. Choose a short mantra for your first one, using the list in this book or a mantra that just comes to mind. Place a clock in sight so that you won't be distracted by wondering how long you have meditated. You can sit in a chair or on the floor, cross your legs or not. You can also stand, kneel, or lie down. Choose the position that seems most natural to you. Once settled, note the time and simply begin to repeat the mantra in your mind (or out loud if you wish) over and over.

Meditation is a gentle art. If you strain to concentrate, it just doesn't work. When you find your mind wandering, you should never let it disturb you, but just gently turn back to the chosen words. Anxiety to succeed is the most frequent difficulty people encounter while learning to use a mantra. I am oversimplifying, but in part any kind of meditation is like giving your mind a vacation. Not a vacation of sleep or daydreaming, but a vacation where relaxation is achieved by concentrating on something far removed from your mind's usual daily round of decision making. In the words of St. Francis de Sales: "Go on in all simplicity; do not be so anxious to win a quiet mind, and it will be all the quieter."

Depending on your personality, your general state of mind, and your immediate mood, you may find it easy or difficult to learn to meditate. Fifteen or twenty minutes is a good length of time to repeat a mantra, yet at the start even five minutes may seem endless. The first few times you try to meditate, it may merely result in a seesaw for attention between the mantra and your wandering thoughts. Unlike natural meditation, a method must be learned, and like any learning process, this requires discipline. Meditate once or twice a day (early mornings and late afternoons are good times). A help to both learning and discipline is to meditate with others. This need not be daily, but a planned hour set aside each week for meditation with a few friends, followed by discussion, can often speed the learning process tremendously.

The goal of *secular* meditation is to achieve a state of mind that is both relaxed and aware. Christian meditation has the further goal of listening to God, and here again we face the danger of trying too hard. A delicate balance is required. One must have a certain sense that this is holy time without having any concern that something "should" happen

BE
STILL

AND KNOW THAT I AM
GOD

or that "If I don't get a message from God, I must not be doing it right." (If you are thinking anything of the kind, you are *not* doing it right!) George Macdonald wrote a sentence that seems very pertinent here: "There is such a thing as a sacred idleness, the cultivation of which is now fearfully neglected." It is in such an idleness that we may hear God, who has been there, waiting for us all along. As F. W. Faber said:

> There is hardly ever a complete silence in our soul. God is whispering to us well-nigh incessantly. Whenever the sounds of the world die out in the soul, or sink low, then we hear these whisperings of God. He is always whispering to us, only we do not always hear, because of the noise, hurry, and distraction which life causes as it rushes on.

One of the major differences between secular and Christian meditation is that whereas secular meditation calls for mantras that are neutral or meaningless, Christian mantras are full to overflowing with meaning. Here is another delicate balance, for I am definitely not saying that mantras are subjects for intellectual speculation. One *could,* of course, spend a lifetime in theological research and study, taking a mantra such as: "In him we live and move and have our being." One could also spend an hour in deliberate consideration of its meaning. But if we did, it would bear small resemblance to meditation.

A certain kind of Christian meditation has been called intellectual meditation, but when used, correctives are soon suggested. In 1534 Martin Luther wrote a description of meditating on the Lord's Prayer which includes words of great beauty and clarity that describe both listening to God and hearing God. He was writing about intellectual meditation, but said that often he came "into such richness of thought" that he went no further with the words but let them "slip away to give the thoughts room and to listen in silence . . . For there the Holy Spirit itself speaks, and of its speech a word is better than a thousand prayers of ours."

The medieval mystic, Meister Eckhart, wrote: "The very best and utmost of attainment in this life is to remain still and let God act and speak in thee." In those last words to "let God act and speak in thee," there lies a key: Christian meditative practice uses meaningful statements as a springboard for meditation, but then it lets God guide the thoughts. The mind that God made is given back to us to use as we wish, whether it is to lead us from thought to thought or into that stillness where, without words, we suddenly perceive, sense, or understand in a new way.

The two greatest difficulties that hinder us from learning any type of Christian meditation are caused by the two areas that I have just described: We need to adopt a healthy discipline without becoming too anxious to succeed, and we need to meditate on words of great meaning without becoming caught up in intellectual speculation.

Often, a meditation will begin with our repeating a mantra and then losing it to other thoughts, returning to the mantra and losing it again. But after a while, the words become more and more central, more *present,* not just in time, but in quality. We begin to savor the words, to feel their meanings and the meaning beyond meanings. As the turmoil of our thoughts gives way to quietness, the words become alive in our hearts and minds. In writing of meditation, E. Herman said: "At first the whole Spiritual world seems a vague abstraction, but gradually, . . . what was vague and empty is seen to be a full and wonderfully articulated reality . . . We become familiar with the infinite riches of the many-sided idea which is God."

In speaking of long use of the Jesus prayer, Louis Bouyer quotes from and refers to *The Philokalia* (spiritual writings from the Eastern Church, dating from the fourth to the fourteenth century):

> By it the mind is purified and unified, with the result that our thoughts "play within it as fishes play and dolphins leap in a calm sea." This effect comes about little by little. At first the name of Jesus is the lamp that lightens our darkness; later it becomes a full moon in the sky of our heart; finally, it is the rising sun. Then a dialogue with Christ begins, in which he, having become the master of our heart, makes his will known to it.

A great deal has been written about meditation and breathing. Buddhist meditative methods sometimes ask you to concentrate on your normal breathing and nothing else. Breathing exercises are an integral part of Hatha Yoga, and it is sometimes suggested that the Jesus prayer be synchronized with breathing. Of all this, I will say little because simplicity and common sense seem to me to be the best approach.

Any exercises involving deep breathing or holding your breath fall outside the scope of this book because although sometimes used by Christians in association with meditation, they are not common Christian practice. If you wish, you may read something of them in Dechanet's *Christian Yoga*. On the other hand, the synchronization of a mantra with your normal breathing pattern is something that comes about naturally. The mantra simply falls into step with the regular rhythm of your breathing. When you are having difficulties quieting the turmoil in your mind, it helps if you concentrate simultaneously on your breathing as well as your mantra. The words must be ones that fit well with your pattern of breathing, and for this purpose the shorter mantras are usually best.

The use of mantras need not be restricted to a particular time and place. Certain types of work and exercise have rhythms that lend themselves to repeating mantras. In natural meditation the simple activity is the only subject occupying the foreground of your mind. I am now suggesting a double concentration on mantra and activity. Of all types of such simple activity suitable for use with a mantra, the most common and one of the best is walking. You may experiment with any of the mantras previously listed and see which seems best to fit your pace. If you are walking on a beautiful country path, so much the better, but a dreary city pavement can take on a new dimension when walked to the high tune of words of worship and remembrance.

Whether there is a rhythm to an activity or not, mantras have often been employed by Christians while they worked at simple tasks. Eighteen centuries ago, Lucius, an early monk, said:

> I will show you that I do not stop praying while I work. I am there, seated with God, and when I set my little leaves to soak and when I weave rope from them, I say "Have mercy on me, O God, in the greatness of your goodness, wipe away my sins in the multitude of your mercies." Now, is this not praying?

FREELY

YOU

HAVE

RECEIVED

FREELY  GIVE

Prince Vladimir Monomach was a Russian prince, but do not be misled by the title. Vladimir lived a life of simplicity, hard work, and prayer. For the benefit of his sons he wrote a book called *Admonition,* and one of his suggestions to them was the following:

> When you are riding on horseback and have no business conversation with anyone, if you know no other prayers, call: "Lord, have mercy," unceasingly and secretly: that prayer is best of all, better than thinking of nonsense while riding.

Some mantras seem natural ones to use while working such as: "Serve the Lord with gladness and come before his presence with a song." Or if doing an unpleasant or boring task: "Surely the Lord is in this place and I knew it not."

The writer of the following quotation does not need to remind herself that "the Lord is in this place." They are the words of an anonymous woman who lived in poverty in the eighteenth century:

> I do not know when I have had happier times in my soul, than when I have been sitting at work, with nothing before me but a candle and a white cloth, and hearing no sound but that of my own breath, with God in my soul and heaven in my eye . . . I rejoice in being exactly what I am,—a creature capable of loving God, and who, as long as God lives, must be happy. I get up and look for a while out of the window, and gaze at the moon and stars, the work of an Almighty hand. I think of the grandeur of the universe, and then sit down, and think myself one of the happiest beings in it.

TAKE

MY YOKE

UPON YOU

AND LEARN OF ME

Mantras, as we said earlier, should either be the word *God* or imply God, but there are special occasions when repeating words that are not as directly God-centered may be useful. A few examples speak for themselves:

Consecrate yourself today to the Lord.

The Lord your God is with you wherever you go.

Be strong and of good courage.

Set a watch, O Lord, before my mouth; keep the door of my lips.

Judge not, that ye be not judged.

Love your enemies, bless them that curse you.

Be not overcome of evil, but overcome evil with good.

Truly this is a grief, and I must bear it.

Let not your heart be troubled, neither let it be afraid.

When I sit in darkness, the Lord shall be my light.

Therefore endure hardness, as a good soldier of Jesus Christ.

Acquaint now thyself with him, and be at peace.

It is easy to see by their content how many of the foregoing verses could be used. Often they may calm your spirit when you are facing something fearful, or turn your heart when it is caught up in feelings you wish to change. You may simply repeat a verse a few times before an event. As you are coming home: *Peace be to this house*. Or you may return to a verse each time the thought you wished to vanish again assaults your heart and mind: *Be ye kind to one another*.

Speaking very simply, George Macdonald once wrote:

> You have a disagreeable duty to do at twelve o'clock. Do not blacken nine, and ten, and eleven, and all between, with the color of twelve. Do the work of each, and reap your reward in peace. So when the dreaded moment in the future becomes the present, you shall meet it walking in the light, and that light will overcome its darkness.

We all know such times, and often it is more than a disagreeable duty we face. I remember once when a man who had come to me for spiritual advice unexpectedly appeared in my yard. I knew that he had been in and out of mental hospitals for years, but I had never seen him when he was more than mildly disturbed. I had grown to believe that God might help him where doctors had failed, and eventually God did help him. But at that moment I could hear him talking and singing to himself in a loud voice. I am not a trained therapist, I was alone, he was a strong man and obviously out of his mind. I was frightened. Yet I did not feel that I should call the police or his family before speaking to him. It was as if he were asking: "Do Christians really care?" I remember instinctively starting to say to myself: "Perfect love casteth out fear. Perfect love casteth out fear . . . ," as I walked downstairs and out into the yard.

IV

FROM
ANCIENT ROOTS
Meditation and
Christian Worship

When you look at traditional services of Christian worship in search of opportunities for meditation, certain things leap into the foreground that you had never noticed before and other matters recede as of lesser importance. Think, for instance, of the practice of waiting upon the Spirit in silence, so well illustrated by a Quaker meeting. Surely all Christian services could use more silence, particularly those denominations that have recently revised or translated their liturgies or services of Sunday worship. Few articles on new liturgies mention their inevitable (if temporary) effect on meditation. There you are in church, quietly loving and listening to God through familiar words, and suddenly you stumble . . . some of the words you were saying so lovingly have been changed, phraseology is different, or a new prayer has been substituted for an old one, and you are abruptly pulled back from prayer to hunt for the right line in the order of service.

Another kind of silence is not really silence at all but the relative peace provided by a language you do not understand. An article by Douglas Brown, speaking of the translation of the Roman Catholic mass from Latin, referred to the loss of "that blessed silence." I am not trying to make an argument for or against new language in liturgical churches but merely stating that until new words are as familiar as old, the need for periods of silence for the congregation to meditate is even greater than usual. In the early Church, periods of silence during worship were customary. Describing part of an early liturgy, Duchesne in *Christian Worship* writes:

> Then silence falls. The faithful take up the attitude of prayer: standing, with lifted arms and outstretched hands. On certain days they kneel, or prostrate themselves with their faces to the ground. Thus they remain for a time praying in silence. Then the voice of the leader is heard gathering up in a few words the prayers which have issued from all hearts; and the congregation united itself with his action by replying Amen.

One of the major arguments given for liturgical changes and for new translations of the Bible is that we must understand what we are saying and reading. This seems only common sense. But if, in the process, we crowd out all chance to hear what *God* is saying, then something is dreadfully wrong. Somehow time for inner silence must be preserved.

When we turn again to look at traditional services with eyes searching for meditative practices, perhaps the greatest shift in focus comes when we pause to consider the significance of some of the most common and familiar words said in our churches. Although these words are not repeated as often as mantras, there is a distinct relationship. Known by heart and repeated Sunday after Sunday in services blessed by sacraments and by common worship, they are clearly meditative in nature.

Whether it is in those denominations dedicated to formal liturgies or in those which believe in more spontaneous expression, the use of one or several words in response to priest or preacher is well-nigh universal. Probably the two words most commonly employed in this way are *alleluia* and *amen*.

It is hard to think of such short responses as being meditative, yet taken within the context of a service, it becomes clearer. If Christian worshippers are already caught up in the words of the service, their response is a dedication, a joining in. It is almost as if each heart said to God: "I'm listening."

Amen and alleluia have something else in common: They are untranslated from the original Hebrew. *Amen* is a Hebrew word used to express assent to what has been said. It could be translated as "truly." But the fact remains that this Old Testament word is *not* translated in our worship and neither is *alleluia*. (When one uses the variant spelling *hallelujah,* its Hebrew origin is easy to see as the word means "praise ye God," or "praise ye Yah," and *Yah* is an abbreviated form of the Hebrew word for God: *Yahweh.*)

Did these words remain untranslated just because they were short? Perhaps, but it also seems likely that they meant so much to the early Jewish Christians that the feeling poured into them was conveyed to the later converts who spoke Greek and Latin. With these two words, their meaning becomes more a matter of feeling than of intellectual understanding. The fact that many of us may not even know that alleluia means "praise ye God" does not mean that our hearts may not be shouting with joy in the Lord as we say or sing: "Alleluia!"

In gathering material for this book I've found myself often moved by a dual realization: the great antiquity of some of the words still said today and the fact that they are shared by millions of Christians of many denominations. Divided as we are, we do not have a chance to realize where we are united. For instance, "Lift up your hearts" and "We lift them up to the Lord" are some of the most universally spoken words in Christian worship today, and yet they were mentioned by Cyprian as early as 252 and by Hippolytus possibly as early as 197. These words are usually followed by two other sentences which are even older as they derive from a Jewish Benediction. Whatever the exact translation, the awesome truth remains that for thousands of years people have helped each other to worship God by repeating these sentences:

> Lift up your hearts.
> *We lift them up to the Lord.*
>
> Let us give thanks to the Lord our God.
> *It is right to give him thanks and praise.*

The greeting, "The Lord be with you," and the response, "And with thy spirit," are also ancient. It was in common use among the Jews, and an example may be found in the Book of Ruth where Boaz said to the reapers, "The Lord be with you." And they answered him, "The Lord bless thee." In slightly varying forms this salutation and response became and have remained a part of Christian worship. They formed the greeting of the priest and people as they began the celebration of the Lord's Supper in the early years of the Christian Church. They served—and still serve—as a reminder to priest and congregation that they worship with Christ and with each other.

THE
LORD
BE
WITH YOU

AND

WITH

THY

SPIRIT

Whether you actually use liturgical sentences in a meditative fashion or not depends to a large extent on why you, and those around you, attend church. Whatever your denomination and even if you are unused to any regular liturgy, imagine for a moment that *you and everyone around you have gathered together for the sole purpose of worshipping God*. Within this context the minister says the words we quoted earlier: "Lift up your hearts!" In unison the congregation replies with one heart and many voices, "We lift them up to the Lord." Then the priest or minister says: "Let us give thanks to the Lord our God," and the congregation responds, "It is right to give him thanks and praise." Repetition aids meditation, but it is not the only aid: Dedication of the time, openness of heart and mind, and the context in which one meditates are of even greater importance.

In William James's classic, *Varieties of Religious Experience,* he said something that seems pertinent to liturgical sentences and indeed to this whole book: "The simplest rudiment of mystical experience would seem to be that deepened sense of the significance of a maxim or formula which occasionally sweeps over one." Who has not at sometime known such a "deepened sense of the significance" of familiar words from Bible or liturgy?

The liturgical sentences we have quoted have spoken for and to Christians down through the centuries. Although sometimes used in other church services, their origin and present use is primarily in that service and sacrament in which we celebrate our Lord's Last Supper. Nomenclature varies from denomination to denomination. The word *liturgy* is often used, but liturgy also can be interpreted to mean any service of worship. However it is titled—the Mass, the Liturgy, our Lord's Supper, the Eucharist, or the Holy Communion—and whether it is frequently or infrequently celebrated, it is, with Baptism, the most universal of all Christian services and sacraments. It expresses and conveys the central realities of the Christian faith.

To give some idea of how such responsive sentences appear within the context of a liturgy, I quote portions of *The Liturgy of the Faithful* of the Greek Orthodox Church.

Peace be unto all.
And with thy spirit.

Let us love one another, that we may with one mind confess:
The Father, Son and Holy Spirit, Trinity, one is essence and undivided.
The doors, the doors; in wisdom let us attend.
(Everyone then joins in saying the creed.)

Let us stand aright; let us stand in awe; let us attend,
that we may make the Holy Offering in peace.
A mercy of peace, a sacrifice of praise.
The Grace of our Lord Jesus Christ, and the love of God the Father, and the communion of the Holy Spirit be with you all.
And with thy spirit.
Let us lift up our hearts.
We lift them up unto the Lord.
Let us give thanks unto the Lord.
It is meet and right.

(The following Communion Anthem comes later in the liturgy.)

Praise ye the Lord from the Heavens. Alleluia.
Praise ye the Lord from the Heavens. Alleluia.
Praise ye the Lord from the Heavens. Alleluia.

The Communion Anthem just quoted brings up another meditative aspect of church services: repetition. Not merely repeating the same sentences once in each service but repeating them within the service. One of the best known and best loved of these is the repetition of the word *Holy* within the short anthem often referred to as The Sanctus. It is said or sung after quite a bit of the service has already passed, and there is often an almost tangible sense of the congregation gathering their personal thoughts into one thought as they cry out to heaven:

LORD GOD OF HOSTS
HEAVEN & EARTH ARE
FULL OF THY GLORY

GLORY BE TO THEE
O LORD MOST HIGH

BLESSED IS HE WHO
COMES IN THE NAME
OF THE LORD

HOSANNA
IN THE HIGHEST

The short prayer, "Lord have mercy upon us," is commonly called the *Kyrie Eleison* or, more briefly, the *Kyrie,* and it is often still said or sung in Greek as it must have been in the early Church when Greek was the common language. Sometimes it is shortened to *Lord have mercy,* while other denominations add *Christ have mercy.*

The *Kyrie* is repeated three or more times. This is referred to as threefold, sevenfold, ninefold, etc. Often, perhaps because of particularly beautiful musical settings, churches will employ a greater number of "folds" than are actually called for in their liturgies.

> Lord, have mercy upon us.
> *Lord, have mercy upon us.*
> Christ, have mercy upon us.
> *Christ, have mercy upon us.*
> Lord, have mercy upon us.
> *Lord, have mercy upon us.*

Caught up in repeating the prayer we seldom stop to wonder *why* we say it again and again. Are we so unsure of God's mercy? It would seem more likely that saying the same words over and over helps to open our hearts and minds *to hear and receive* his mercy. Perhaps no part of traditional church services so clearly leaves room for listening prayer. The words we say to Christ are the vehicle for our hearing him.

The *Kyrie* was originally a part of an early litany. Litanies are a series of sentences, said by the priest or minister, which describe the needs of the people. The congregation responds employing a short prayer of assent. The great traditional litanies are all-inclusive in nature. Like beads on a string, the whole range of human hopes and fears are brought before the Lord in prayer. In the Middle Ages many new litanies were written, but instead of their being incorporated into the service, these litanies were used in procession and for special occasions: to bless the fields and orchards, in time of calamity, and in time of thanksgiving.

Martin Luther regarded the litany as "next to the holy Lord's Prayer the very best that has come to earth" and restored a simplified, traditional form to a regular position in the liturgy. Today there is a new interest in litanies among a number of denominations. Some modern litanies are general and all-inclusive, while others are for a particular purpose. Here is an abridged portion of a modern Presbyterian litany for the nation:

> LEADER: Help us to repent our country's wrong, and to choose your right in reunion and renewal.
>
> PEOPLE: *Amen.*
>
> LEADER: Teach us peace, so that we may plow up battlefields and pound weapons into building tools, and learn to talk across old boundaries as brothers in your love.
>
> PEOPLE: *Great God, renew this nation.*
>
> LEADER: Talk sense to us, so that we may wisely end all prejudice, and may put a stop to cruelty, which divides or wounds the human family.
>
> PEOPLE: *Great God, renew this nation.*
>
> LEADER: Draw us together as one people who do your will, so that our land may be a light to nations, leading the way to your promised kingdom, which is coming among us.
>
> PEOPLE: *Amen.*

No matter how moving and pertinent the new litanies may be, the following selections from the fourth-century litany attributed to St. John Chrysostom still speak for us today:

> Blessed be the kingdom of the Father, the Son and
> the Holy Ghost, now and forever, world without end.
> *Amen.*
>
> In time of peace, let us pray to the Lord:
> *Lord, have mercy on us.*
>
> For the peace from on high and for the salvation of our
> souls, let us pray to the Lord:
> *Lord, have mercy on us.*

For the peace of the whole world, for the good estate
of all the Holy Churches of God, and for the unity of all,
let us pray to the Lord:
Lord, have mercy on us.

For this holy House and for those who enter therein with
faith, reverence and fear of God, let us pray to the Lord:
Lord, have mercy on us.

For this land, and for every city and country and for all
the faithful who dwell therein, let us pray to the Lord:
Lord, have mercy on us.

For a good state of climate, abundance of the fruits of the
earth, and peaceful seasons, let us pray to the Lord:
Lord, have mercy on us.

For sailors, travelers, the sick, sufferers, prisoners,
for the salvation of all, let us pray to the Lord:
Lord, have mercy on us.

That we may be delivered from all affliction, wrath,
peril and need, let us pray to the Lord:
Lord, have mercy.

Help, save, pity, and guard us, O God, by Thy Grace:
Lord, have mercy on us.

V

MUSIC AND
MEDITATION

Music by itself is a universal aid to meditation. We can be caught up into another world as we listen to ancient chanting, medieval plainsong, a classic symphony, the popular songs of the times, or the rhythmic beat of drums. When words are set to music, it not only makes it easier to learn them by heart, but is often—although not always—an aid to meditation.

Under certain circumstances, music may be a distraction rather than an aid to meditation. For instance, it is difficult, if not impossible, to meditate on a mantra if a rhythm other than your inner one assaults the ears. Noise of other kinds can more easily be shut out of your mind, but a rhythmical tune insistently beats its way in. To meditate to music, you have to join it. If it is, for instance, a great chorale or symphony, you can inwardly dedicate your listening and let the deeper mind drift as in natural meditation. But if it is a melodic hymn, or the familiar setting for liturgical responses, it is best to sing with all your being. Here—as with the introduction of new words in a liturgy—tunes that you do not know, and cannot easily sing, hinder meditation. I do not mean by this that I am against new music! But *from the point of view of meditation,* new music should either be easy for the congregation to learn, or else music to which they need only listen and in which they may lose themselves in meditation.

It helps to give us perspective to look at several periods in history where music played a particularly important part in the life of the Church, and—in different ways—provided a vehicle for meditation.

For the first three hundred years, the Church was outlawed and persecuted. Small groups met in secret and yet they sang. This was "to a large extent, a spontaneous congregational activity." In two of his letters, St. Paul gives us a sense of the early Christian attitude towards singing. To the young church in Ephesus he wrote: "Be filled with the Spirit, addressing one another in psalms and hymns and spiritual songs, singing and making melody to the Lord with all your heart." And in words that clearly indicate the meditative nature of the singing, he wrote to Corinth: "I will pray with the Spirit, and I will pray with the understanding also. I will sing with the Spirit, and I will sing with the understanding also."

These earliest Christians sang psalms and chants as they had been sung in the synagogue, gradually adding Christian prayers and songs. Responsive sentences were also sung, and many of these, as we have

just seen, were of Jewish origin. But as converts from different cultures increased, so did musical variety, until each congregation had its own music. When persecution finally ceased and Christians could meet more easily, they realized a need and worked towards some "semblance of musical unity."

Here in the early Church two opposing ideals that have appeared and reappeared through the centuries are clearly seen: the joyful spontaneity of the worshipper singing in his own language and music, and the need for a common way of worship familiar to all Christians.

This common way, or rather two common ways—Eastern and Western—came to its greatest flowering in the West during the Middle Ages. While only the educated minority fully understood the language of worship, a tremendous aid to meditation existed in those centuries which we have lost today: Within the Christian world there was a deep and well-nigh universal faith.

Even today we cannot think of the Middle Ages without thinking of cathedrals, but imagine how it must have been then: You were an unlettered peasant in a time when life was hard and death ever at hand. With faith in God and surrounded by others who also had faith, you entered a cathedral. No skyscrapers overwhelmed it. It was far taller than any building you had ever seen or dreamed of. In all probability you and your friends had cut and hauled stones to the site yourselves. Or

perhaps you were an artist and artisan and had carved those stones or created windows or mosaics. In either case, it was the story of Christianity told in stone and glass, rather than in words, that gave you and your fellow worshippers the most readily available material for meditation. And in the background there was music. In the words of Will Durant:

> We have done the cathedral injustice. It was not the cold and empty tomb that the visitor enters today. It functioned . . . It received the monks or canons who many times each day stood in the choir stalls and sang the canonical Hours. It heard the importunate litanies of congregations seeking divine mercy and aid . . . Its great spaces echoed solemnly with the music of the Mass. And the music was as vital as the church edifice itself, more deeply stirring than all the glory of glass or stone.

Hymns in Greek and Latin were sung and composed both before and during the Middle Ages. One of the greatest and oldest of these is still known by its Latin title *Gloria in Excelsis,* but is actually of Greek origin. It is a series of acclamations and petitions, practically all of them biblically based and familiar from other parts of Christian worship. Here they are put together as a Christian psalm, the repeated thoughts gaining in strength and power as one follows the other.

Glory be to God on high and on earth peace, good will towards men. We praise thee, we bless thee, we worship thee, we give thanks to thee for thy great glory, O Lord God, heavenly King, God the Father Almighty.

O Lord, the only-begotten Son, Jesus Christ; O Lord God, Lamb of God, Son of the Father, that takest away the sin of the world, have mercy upon us. Thou that takest away the sin of the world, receive our prayer. Thou that sittest at the right hand of God the Father, have mercy upon us.

For thou only art holy; thou only art the Lord; thou only, O Christ, with the Holy Ghost, art most high in the glory of God the Father. Amen.

Traditions have a way of becoming "sanctified," and the older they are, the more this is true. By the time of the early Reformation years the idea that the Bible and the words of Christian worship might be translated into a language people could understand was a frightening and heretical thought. Many early translators were condemned and executed. Wycliffe's bones were dug up and burned half a century after his death. Tyndale and John Huss were burnt at the stake. Whether Luther was a greater man, or only the right man at the right time and place, only God knows. It remains that it was Martin Luther who brought the work of these martyrs to fruition.

Luther's own translation of the New Testament was printed in 1522. But Luther did much more than translate. In the words of Louis Bouyer, a French Roman Catholic scholar:

> He brought back a piety directly inspired by the Bible, and diffused it among the common people, who, we suspect, had never seen anything like it since patristic times.

And in the words of Albert Bailey, a New England Congregationalist:

> When Luther nailed his ninety-five theses to the door of the Wittenberg castle church in 1517 he started something besides a Reformation: it was a beginning of a new Hymnody in the vernacular to be sung freely by all the people.

Two centuries later the Methodist movement began in England, a movement where theology, hymns, teaching, prayer, and meditation were almost inextricably interlaced. John Wesley and his brother Charles were Anglican clergymen who preached a rousing, prayerful, and demanding Christianity at a time when the Church of England seemed more interested in sedate services for the landed gentry. When forbidden the pulpits the Wesleys took to the fields, to the prisons, and to the homes of the poor. Their success was phenomenal—but therefore threatening to the established ways—and they and their followers were "stoned, mauled, ducked, hounded with bulldogs, threatened; homes looted, businesses ruined." Eventually the Methodists separated from the Church of England, but both the Wesleys remained Anglicans until their deaths.

In the end it was the hymns that triumphed. The simple, strong, devout teachings of the Wesleys entered church doors—Anglican and many others—through the hymns of Charles Wesley. It seems almost impossible to believe, but Charles wrote 6,500 hymns. Among many denominations—over two centuries later—such hymns as "Jesus, Lover of my soul," "Christ whose glory fills the skies," "Come thou long-expected Jesus," and "Hark the herald angels sing" are familiar and beloved. But it is instructive to look back to where they began.

The following imaginative reconstruction of a Methodist class meeting in Kingswood, in the coal country of England, has been abridged from Albert Bailey's superb book, *The Gospel in Hymns:*

The room is a small school building. The evening is Wednesday, after dark and after supper. Cennick, the leader, is there first; he lights the candles, builds a fire in the grate. Soon the people arrive: an old lady with a cane, a couple of miners in their heavy boots and rough smocks, the grime not wholly removed from hands and face; the town simpleton who longs for company; the village drunk recently snatched from the burning; a carter, a shepherd, a farmer and wife. Most of them cannot read or write and every last one of them is poor—some of them desperately poor; they have worked all their lives and have never been farther away from home than Bristol (four miles). Of such is the Kingdom of God in Kingswood.

Cennick greets them as they come in: "The Lord bless you, brother." "Thank the Lord you could come, sister." "How's the sick girl, Mrs. Stow?" "How's the lamb that broke her leg, Danny?" They nod to one another as they take their seats on the benches, glad to feel the warmth of friendship and a common aspiration. Cennick strikes up an old familiar hymn by Charles Wesley, "O for a thousand tongues." The tune is lively, Cennick is a good singer, everybody joins whether he can sing or not.

The leader then says that Mr. Charles Wesley wrote a new hymn for them when he heard of the stoning of some of the members of the class last week, and the setting on fire of Mr. Barrow's hay-rick by the same ruffians. From his Bible Cennick takes a piece of paper on which are written in Mr. Wesley's own hand the words of "O Thou, to whose all-searching sight."

"It is to be sung in times of trouble and persecution, says Mr. Wesley, and he wrote it especially for us."

Cennick then reads the whole hymn, then re-reads the first stanza and sings it, he re-reads the first two lines and asks them to try to sing them with him. And so on till the first two stanzas have been rehearsed. "That is enough for tonight. We shall tackle the other stanzas on Sunday evening."

The leader then turns to the subject of the evening. "What should a Christian do if he falls into sin?" —that is, "backslides." The subject has been announced at the previous meeting and everybody has been thinking about it. Cennick introduced the subject by reading Charles Wesley's hymn, "Depth of mercy, can there be," which he had taught them to say by heart on previous occasions. He then explained it line by line, and from the Bible read the verses that said the same thing. The talk was a kind of running commentary on the hymn and the Bible and the infinite mercy of God.

At first glance this moving account of early Methodism would seem to have little to do with meditation, but in fact, it has a great deal to do with it. Charles Wesley's thinking about the stoning and writing a hymn was meditative in itself. (All hymns are essentially the fruit of meditation.) What Cennick was doing was giving illiterate people material for Christian meditation and—with the hymns—a vehicle through which they could meditate.

The stories and theology of the Bible speak strongly to and for an enslaved and oppressed people. Under slavery, American Negroes composed some of the strongest, most beautiful, and most meditative Christian songs in existence.

Although the subjects were Christian and the setting slavery, the strong influence of African music is clear. James Weldon Johnson writes of "the form so common to African songs" of employing "leading lines and response." And further: "The solitary voice of the leader is answered by a sound like a rolling sea. The effect produced is strangely moving."

Swing low, sweet chariot,
Comin' for to carry me home.
Swing low, sweet chariot,
Comin' for to carry me home.
I look over Jordan, and what do I see?
Comin' for to carry me home.
A band of angels comin' after me,
Comin' for to carry me home.

FOR TO CARRY ME HOME

FOR TO CARRY ME HOME

FOR TO CARRY ME HOME

FOR TO CARRY ME HOME

Among less familiar spirituals is "I couldn't hear nobody pray," one of the most poignant descriptions of spiritual loneliness I know.

> An' I couldn't hear nobody pray,
> O, Lord, I couldn't hear nobody pray,
> O, Lord, O, way down yonder by myself,
> An' I couldn't hear nobody pray,
>
> In de valley, I couldn't hear nobody pray,
> On a my knees—I couldn't hear nobody pray,
> Wid my burden, I couldn't hear nobody pray,
> An' a my Savior I couldn't hear nobody pray,
>
> O, Lord, an' I couldn't hear nobody pray,
> O, Lord, I couldn't hear nobody pray,
> O, Lord, O, way down yonder by myself,
> An' I couldn't hear nobody pray,
>
> In a to Canaan I couldn't hear nobody pray,
> Troubles am over I couldn't hear nobody pray,
> In de Kingdom I couldn't hear nobody pray,
> Wid a my Jesus, I couldn't hear nobody pray,
>
> O, Lord, an' I couldn't hear nobody pray,
> O, Lord, I couldn't hear nobody pray,
> O, Lord, O way down yonder by myself,
> An' I couldn't hear nobody pray.

Some Negro spirituals were not only sung in church but found their way into the fields and wherever singing could accompany work. There are times in most of our lives today when we could sing spirituals or other hymns as we work. Particularly when the turmoil in our mind is great, when natural meditation turns to worry and mantras flee from our minds, the simple tune and words of a spiritual song may lift our hearts and minds to a quieter plane.

> He's got the whole world in His hands,
> He's got the whole world in His hands,
> He's got the whole world in His hands,
> He's got the whole world in His hands.

IN
HIS
HANDS

Whenever there is a resurgence of the Spirit in people's hearts, they tend to pour forth their prayers and praises in new words and new music. Yet often new music and new songs are resisted. After the coronation of Queen Elizabeth I of England, Protestant exiles came home in great numbers, but from Calvin's Geneva they brought one thing Queen Elizabeth detested: the singing of psalms set to metrical tunes. Elizabeth disparagingly called these "Geneva jiggs." But "singing in her reign became almost a passion, an orgy, and psalms were roared aloud not only in church, but in every street," and eventually Elizabeth herself joined the popular movement and tried her hand at translating psalms into English.

If today we find ourselves either resisting new music or trying to introduce it to a resistant congregation, it is helpful to remind ourselves of the meditative aspects of music. As I said earlier, music which is beyond the ability of the average congregation to sing may be *listened* to in a meditative fashion, but for congregational singing the simpler the tune and the faster it is learned, the greater opportunity they will have to "sing with the Spirit."

O SING UNTO THE LORD A NEW SONG

It is hard to look at one's own time and see where it is going, to sift the merely innovative from the leading of the Spirit and resistance to change from a true desire to worship God. But in Christian music today as in other forms of Christian worship, there are some haunting similarities to the days of the early Church. We too play music to the Lord in the voices of many different cultures. And while we have a respect for diversity, we are also beginning to share our inheritance. In Roman Catholic churches you may hear the strong words of Martin Luther's "A Mighty Fortress is our God," Methodist hymns are sung in churches that once condemned them, and Negro spirituals are finding a larger and larger place in Christian worship of many denominations. There is a coming together of differing traditions, and each is enriched by the other. Nowhere is this more clearly illustrated than when, in a liturgically oriented church, people walk slowly to the altar while choir and congregation quietly sing the spiritual "When I Fall on My Knees."

Let us break bread together, on our knees.
Let us break bread together, on our knees.
When I fall on my knees,
With my face to the rising sun,
O Lord have mercy on me.

Let us drink wine together, on our knees.
Let us drink wine together, on our knees.
When I fall on my knees,
With my face to the rising sun,
O Lord have mercy on me.

Let us praise God together, on our knees.
Let us praise God together, on our knees.
When I fall on my knees,
With my face to the rising sun,
O Lord have mercy on me.

WHEN I FALL
ON MY KNEES

In general there seem to be three marks shown by the spiritual songs that are popular today, and they are all qualities useful for meditation: They are apt to be melodic, simple, and stress repetition.

A number of popular songs of this generation are slowly making their way into the music of the Church even though some were not written with the Church in mind. I think particularly of Paul Simon's "Bridge Over Troubled Water" and Bob Dylan's "Blowin' in the Wind" with its haunting melody and questions and the repeated refrain: "The answer, my friend, is blowin' in the wind." So it is with the Spirit as Jesus said so long ago to Nicodemus: "The wind blows where it wills and you hear the sound of it, but you do not know where it comes from nor where it goes."

"I'd like to end this chapter with a modern spiritual song, "The Lord of the Dance." The words and arrangement (from an old Shaker melody) are by Sydney Carter. To some Christians the words may be shocking and to others beautiful. Not only are they meditative in nature for those who find them beautiful, but the whole theme is expressive of the idea of Christian meditation. Words are there and deep meaning is there, and yet they are clearly not meant for intellectual speculation. Nor is the word *Dance* used in an ordinary way. It is an inner and spiritual dance led by Christ. Nothing could be more truly Christian meditation.

I danced in the morning when the world was begun, and I danced in the moon and the stars and the sun, and I came down from heaven and I danced on the earth; at Bethlehem I had my birth.

Dance then wherever you may be. I am the Lord of the Dance, said He. And I'll lead you all wherever you may be, and I'll lead you all in the Dance, said He.

I danced for the scribe and the pharisee, but they would not dance and they wouldn't follow me, I danced for the fisherman for James and John—they came with me and the dance went on.

Dance then wherever you may be. I am the Lord of
the Dance, said He. And I'll lead you all wherever
you may be, and I'll lead you all in the Dance,
said He.

I danced on the Sabbath and I cured the lame. The holy people said it was a shame. They whipped and they stripped and they hung me high, and they left me there on a Cross to die.

Dance then wherever you may be. I am the Lord of
the Dance, said He. And I'll lead you all wherever
you may be, and I'll lead you all in the Dance,
said He.

I danced on a Friday when the sky turned black—it's hard to dance with the devil on your back. They buried my body and they thought I'd gone—but I am the Dance and I still go on.

Dance then wherever you may be. I am the Lord of
the Dance, said He. And I'll lead you all wherever
you may be, and I'll lead you all in the Dance,
said He.

They cut me down and I leapt up high. I am the life that'll never, never die. I'll live in you if you'll live in me. "I am the Lord of the Dance," said He.

Dance then wherever you may be. I am the Lord of
the Dance, said He. And I'll lead you all wherever
you may be, and I'll lead you all in the Dance,
said He.

VI

KNOWN
BY HEART

The words that Mary spoke after she learned that she was to give birth to Jesus can be found in the first chapter of the Gospel of Luke. By themselves they are known as the "Song of Mary" or the "Magnificat." I bring them up not as an example of what *we* know by heart, but of what *Mary* knew. To quote Massey Shepherd, the "Song of Mary" is "a mosaic of allusion and quotation of the whole range of the Old Testament. It could have been composed only by one who was intimately conversant with the Scriptures." How little we know by heart today! A few prayers, an occasional Bible verse, and perhaps a psalm. Very few of us could naturally fall into "a mosaic of allusion and quotation."

The words *to know by heart* have come to mean words that we remember. But when we are speaking of prayer and meditation rather than multiplication tables or Latin grammar, the *by heart* takes an equal place with memory. The Lord's Prayer has probably provided more Christians with an opportunity to listen to God through the words than any other. Yet, on the other hand, no prayer gives a better example of one that can be said by rote rather than by heart. Obviously, other prayers also can be said by rote without paying any attention to either God or the words. It isn't that prayer necessarily means paying strict attention to every word (God may choose to focus our attention on just a few), but as Karl Barth said:

> Prayer must be an act of affection; it is more than a question of using the lips, for God asks the allegiance of our hearts. If the heart is not in it, if it is only a form which is carried out more or less correctly, what is it then?

When we pray with the "allegiance of our hearts," the words are lifted far above those said out of habit and mumbled by rote. They become a song, a lifeline, and a bond of communication between God and man.

Probably the most common form of Christian meditation is a practice that arises so naturally that it is seldom written about. Certainly countless Christians have often centered their thoughts and feelings on a word, a short prayer, or a verse of the Bible. The words may have been consciously chosen, but this is often not a planned method of meditation but rather a movement of the Holy Spirit within a seeking human being. Unbidden, a word or verse comes to mind on awaking. In response you turn it over in your mind slowly, seeing new facets, new meanings. In the middle of the day, it comes back to you, perhaps this time with a sudden insight concerning your own life. After a while you may find yourself purposely bringing it to mind. This may go on for a day or several—or even for many weeks—and then fade away to be replaced perhaps by another word, perhaps by silence.

Such words or phrases are usually ones that may appear simple enough at first glance but reveal innumerable facets as you meditate on them: *growth, faith, forgive them, wisdom, judge not, whole, holy, understanding.* The verses are the kind that you often feel moved to write down and carry in your pocket until you know them by heart. For this reason I call them pocket verses. A pocket verse is not usually repeated constantly but is used for meditation off and on during the day. It is sometimes longer than a mantra and does not have to have a rhythm.

> Imagine: You wake up. The night before you have chosen your sentence. Suddenly you remember it: "*This* is the day that the Lord has made." For a moment your heart leaps. And then you remember what is in store for you this day: Troubles, work, misunderstandings, sorrow, anxiety, pain. You remember the full details and the quite unholy aspects of what lies ahead. But then you come back to the words: "O.K. 'This *is* the day that the Lord has made', but the Lord is still around and so am I. He is with me even now, let's get up and see what we can do with his day."
>
> As you sip your breakfast orange juice, as you read the headlines in the paper, as you go to work, as you deal with people, papers, machines, or whatever you deal with in your work, the sentence keeps coming back: "This is the day that the Lord has made." It wrenches you—not out of the world, but into the world, but the world as seen and lived from another dimension. You become attuned to the possibility of hearing God through everything that you see, everything that happens, everything that you must do.

A pocket verse need not be as central to our faith as a mantra, but it should be capable of revealing many facets. While you mull it over under the different circumstances of the day, the Holy Spirit leads you to see new meanings and new depths of understanding.

You are the salt of the earth.

There was no room for them in the inn.

For where your treasure is,
there will your heart be also.

Faith is the substance of things hoped for,
the evidence of things not seen.

Be ye doers of the word and not hearers only.

Follow me, I will make you fishers of men.

What doth the Lord require of thee, but to do justly
and to love mercy and to walk humbly with thy God?

For he shall give his angels charge over thee,
to keep thee in all thy ways.

You are the temple of God,
and the Spirit of God dwells within you.

Be not conformed to this world: but be ye
transformed by the renewing of your mind.

Take up your cross and follow me.

THERE
WAS NO ROOM FOR
THEM
IN THE INN

Praying with a rosary antedates Christianity. The first recorded Christian use is that of fourth-century monks who repeated the Lord's Prayer many times a day and counted off the prayers on a knotted length of twine. Slowly, such practices became more popular and more complex. By the fifteenth century, the use of the rosary (which takes its name from the Latin *rosarium,* a garden or wreath of roses) became widespread throughout the Christian world.

Modern forms vary but usually include the Hail Mary, the Lord's Prayer, and the Gloria Patri (Glory be to the Father . . .). Meditation on the *mysteries*—major events in the life of Christ or Mary—while repeating the prayers is customary. Here again we see the Christian emphasis on meaning, even if it may be on a larger spiritual meaning than the actual words encompass.

Moslems, Hindus, and Buddhists also use a string of beads as an aid to prayer. There must be a common human need for the use of a rosary to arise as often, and in as many cultures, as it does.

We can all make our own combination of prayers. For instance, you could knot a length of cord with rows of five or ten small knots interspersed with larger ones. As each small knot slips through your fingers say:

> Forgive what we have been
> amend what we are,
> direct what we shall be.

As you come to each large knot, pause and say the following prayer which is based on a portion of Paul's letter to the Ephesians:

> May Christ dwell in our hearts by faith, so that being rooted and grounded in love we may, with all the saints, know that which may not be measured, the length and height and depth of the love of Christ. Amen.

THE
LORD IS
WITH
THEE

Of course, there is no need to use a rosary to meditate on passages that we know by heart. In any pause in our work, or while what we are doing does not absorb all our attention, or when we lie awake in bed, we may quietly listen to God through words we know and love. We all have our favorites, but here are a few good possibilities:

In returning and rest shall you be saved; in quietness and in confidence shall be your strength. *Isa.30:15*

Turn thy mind to the Lord God, from whom life comes: Whereby thou mayest receive His strength, and power to allay all blustering storms and tempests. *George Fox*

For I am persuaded that neither death, nor life, nor angels, nor principalities, nor powers, nor things present, nor things to come, nor height nor depth, nor any other creature, shall be able to separate us from the love of God. *Rom. 8:38–39*

If I take the wings of the morning, and dwell in the uttermost parts of the sea, even there shall thy hand lead me, and thy right hand shall hold me. *Psalm 139:9–10*

Give me the grace to discover and live what you have dreamed for me. *Michel Quoist*

God is our refuge and strength, a very present help in trouble. Therefore we will not fear, though the earth be moved, and the mountains be carried into the midst of the sea. *Psalm 46:1–2*

The kingdom of heaven is like a grain of mustard seed, which a man took, and sowed in his field. It is indeed the least of all seeds, but when grown it becomes like a tree so that the birds of the air come and make nests in its branches. *Matt. 13:31–32*

I said to the man at the gate of the year—"Give me a light that I may tread safely into the unknown." And he replied, "Go out into the darkness and put your hand into the hand of God. That shall be to you better than the light, and safer than a known way." *M. L. Haskin*

The Psalms, more than any other book in the Old Testament, have found a place in Christian hearts. As Evelyn Underhill said, the Psalter was "familiar from childhood to Our Lord and the first generation of disciples, it was taken over without question from temple and synagogue worship by the primitive Church."

John Calvin, writing about the Psalter in the sixteenth century, said:

> I may truly call this book an anatomy of all parts of the soul, for no one can feel a movement of the Spirit which is not reflected in this mirror. All the sorrows, troubles, fears, doubts, hopes, pains, perplexities, and stormy outbreaks by which the hearts of men are tossed, have been depicted here to the very life.

In this century the Trappist monk, Thomas Merton, wrote:

> Those whose vocation in the Church is prayer find that they live on the Psalms—for the Psalms enter into every department of their life. Monks get up to chant Psalms in the middle of the night. They find phrases from the Psalter on their lips at Mass. They interrupt their work in the fields or the workshops of the monastery to sing the Psalms of the day hours. They recite Psalms after their meals and practically the last words on their lips at night are verses written hundreds of years ago by one of the Psalmists.

The Psalms are poetry, but unlike much of the poetry with which we are familiar, they do not use rhyme nor a fixed number of syllables but a more flexible rhythm of stresses and beats. Of greatest importance to the poetry of a psalm is repetition, not so much the repetition of words as the repetition of thoughts. In a beautiful passage that almost sounds like a psalm itself, Mary Ellen Chase describes this aspect of the Psalms:

> The basic literary feature in the Psalms as in all other Hebrew poetry is *repetition*. Their poets in the excess of their feeling want to drive home a truth—a conviction or an assurance, a grievance, a hope, or a joy, a curse or a blessing, a call to praise or a lament. To them, once is not enough. They must say twice what they long to say, or three times, even four in a succession of often tumultuous lines.

Often it is a psalm taken as a whole, or large portions of one, that afford the best illustration of this kind of repetition, such as the following verses from Psalm 42, or both couplets and the whole of Psalm 150. (See pp. 115–127.)

> Like as the hart desires the water-brooks,
> so longs my soul after thee, O God.
>
> My soul is athirst for God, yea, even for the living God.
> When shall I come to appear before the presence of God?
>
> My tears have been my meat day and night,
> while they daily say unto me, "Where is now your God?"
>
> Why are you so full of heaviness, O my soul?
> And why are you so disquieted within me?
> O put your trust in God; for I will yet thank him,
> which is the help of my countenance, and my God.

Deep calls to deep in the noise of thy waterfloods,
all the waves and storms are gone over me.
I will say to God my strength, "Why hast thou forgotten me?
Why go I so heavily, while the enemy oppresses me?"

My bones are smitten asunder as with a sword,
while mine enemies say daily: "Where is now your God?"

Why are you so vexed, O my soul?
and why are you so disquieted within me?
O put your trust in God; for I will yet thank him,
which is the help of my countenance, and my God.

PRAISE YE
THE LORD

PRAISE GOD IN HIS SANCTUARY

PRAISE HIM IN THE FIRMAMENT OF HIS POWER

PRAISE HIM

FOR HIS
MIGHTY ACTS

PRAISE HIM

ACCORDING TO HIS EXCELLENT GREATNESS

PRAISE HIM WITH THE SOUND OF THE TRUMPET

PRAISE HIM WITH THE LUTE AND HARP

PRAISE HIM WITH THE TIMBREL AND DANCE

PRAISE HIM WITH STRINGED INSTRUMENTS AND PIPES

PRAISE HIM
UPON THE
LOUD CYMBALS

PRAISE HIM UPON THE HIGH SOUNDING CYMBALS

LET EVERYTHING THAT HATH BREATH

PRAISE THE LORD

PRAISE YE

THE LORD

EPILOGUE

If Christians have had ways of meditation all along, why have so many had to turn to Hindu, Buddhist, Islamic, or secular methods? A great deal of the answer lies simply in the fact that we had so neglected our spiritual heritage that books about Christian prayer were hard to find. It was often easier to find a guru than a teacher of Christian prayer. Today, interest in Christian spirituality is alive but in a confused and transitional state. We need to look broadly and imaginatively—and with the guidance of the Spirit—at our spiritual resources. Yet the guidance of the Spirit comes through meditation, and only through meditation itself will a clear pattern of a Christian spirituality emerge from the confusion.

To meditate on a regular basis takes dedication and discipline. It is interesting to note that in the past few decades, while the Church has been busily throwing out old spiritual disciplines as archaic, many of the younger generation have left the Church and turned to a variety of gurus to learn strict and ancient spiritual disciplines.

INCLINE YOUR EAR
AND COME UNTO ME

HEAR †††

AND

YOUR SOUL

SHALL LIVE

Dedication and discipline must go hand in hand with love and listening. We may love God a great deal or a very little. What counts is what we do with that love. Do we enjoy it momentarily and then let it evaporate, or do we respond to it? In an evergrowing spiral love calls for dedication, dedication for discipline, discipline for listening, and listening increases our love of God.

The ways in which we may listen to God are simple and available to all. Just to realize what we have and to think about it is a beginning. We can consider all old prayers and songs in a new light and mull over the idea of prayer as a two-way street. We can ask ourselves whether we are so busy saying things to God that we never give him a chance to get a word in edgewise. We can remind ourselves that familiar words we hear and say in church are neither magic passwords nor merely common salutations like "How are you?" which we say by force of habit, but words rich with meaning that can be vehicles for hearing God. We can learn new words and prayers by heart so that they too may become vehicles for meditation. But above all, we can find and use opportunities for meditation.

As we have seen, while meditation is often a solitary occupation, it may also be an integral part of Christian worship. For a church service to become a meditative service, the priest or pastor and the congregation must support each other in their openness to God. This openness to God is the necessary base for all meditation. Given that base, there are many ways in which the clergy may help their congregation to meditate. Sometimes ministers forget what it is like to be in the pew. Such simple things make such a large difference. It is not possible to meditate on words you cannot hear. It is not easy to meditate on words read in an ecclesiastical drone, or too dramatically, or too fast, or as if the words held no more meaning than a shopping list. Surely, the living Word should be read simply, clearly, and as if the reader believed it to be living. There is also the matter of time to listen to God. This doesn't necessarily mean blocks of silence. God may break through to us in a moment. But there must be a quality of peace about that moment. The order of service should either be obvious to all, or clearly announced. No one who is hurrying to find the next hymn has a chance to meditate on the last prayer.

Individual Christians, and whole congregations, lose and regain their attitude of love and listening. This has been true throughout history. Like Martha in the story of Martha and Mary, we are so busy, so "cumbered about with much serving" that we forget to sit at Jesus' feet and listen. We need to remember again.

I think of three sentences from a modern liturgy:

> Christ has died.
> Christ is risen.
> Christ will come again.

These words speak of past, present, and future, but like so many Christian sentences, they have related meanings. One of these meanings is that to some extent all of us are dead to Christ. Yet Christ is not dead. And if we learn to listen to him, and are open to him, he will come again, and more fully, into our lives.

THEY THAT WAIT
UPON THE LORD
SHALL RENEW
THEIR STRENGTH

NOTES

Quotations from the Bible are taken from the King James Version either word for word or slightly abridged or paraphrased. If they have come from another translation we have so indicated in the notes.

PROLOGUE

9 Karl Rahner, *Spiritual Exercises,* (Herder & Herder, 1965.)

Bede Frost, *The Art of Mental Prayer,* (London: SPCK, 1940.)

I

NATURAL MEDITATION AND CHRISTIAN PRAYER

13 Adam Smith, *Powers of the Mind,* (New York: Random House, 1975.)

13 Herbert Benson, *The Relaxation Response,* (New York: Avon Books, 1976.)

17 "The kingdom of God . . ." Luke 17:21.

18 Kathleen Hughes, *The Church in Early Irish Society,* (Cornell University Press, 1966.)

Alexander Carmichael, *Carmina Gadelica,* Vol. I, (Edinburgh: Scottish Academic Press, 1972.)

Alexander Carmichael, *Celtic Invocations: Selections from Vol. I of Carmina Gadelica,* (Noroton: Vineyard Books, 1977.)

19 "Commit thy works . . ." Prov. 16:3.

21 "Remember the sabbath day . . ." Ex. 20:8.

"The sabbath was made . . ." Mark 2:27.

23 "Lord I believe . . ." Mark 9:24.

II

CHRISTIAN MANTRAS

31 Swami Nikhilananda, *Hinduism,* (London: Allen and Unwin, 1959.)

32 Writings from *The Philokalia on Prayer of the Heart,* trans. from the Russian text by E. Kadloubousky and G. E. H. Palmer, (London: Faber and Faber, 1975.)

The Way of A Pilgrim and The Pilgrim Continues His Way, trans. from the Russian by R. M. French, (New York: The Seabury Press, 1965.)

36 "Even so come Lord Jesus." Rev. 22:20.

"The joy of the Lord . . ." Neh. 8:10.

"Thy kingdom come . . ." Matt. 6:10.

"Let every creature . . ." William Law.

"Teach me what . . ." Job 34:32 (RSV).

"We are the temple . . ." II Cor. 6:16.

"Love one another . . ." John 13:34.

"Lose your life to find it." Adapted from Matt. 10:39; 16:25; Mark 8:35; Luke 9:24; John 12:25.

"Prepare the way . . ." Matt. 3:3.

"Hallowed be thy name." Matt. 6:9.

"Behold the Lamb of God." John 1:29.

"If any one thirst . . ." John 7:37 (RSV).

"Once I was blind . . ." John 9:25.

37 "Love one another . . ." John 13:34.

38 "Worship the Lord in the beauty of holiness . . ." Verse 9 of Psalm 96 as used in the Book of Common Prayer (1928) service for Morning Prayer. The portion of Psalm 96 said at this service is usually referred to as the Venite.

"Seek and you shall find . . ." Matt. 7:7.

38 "Bless the Lord, O my soul . . ." Psa. 103:1.

"Thou art the Christ . . ." Matt. 16:16.

"Thine is the kingdom . . ." Matt. 6:13.

"Create in me a clean heart . . ." Psa. 51:10.

"Except a man be born again . . ." John 3:3.

"Holy, holy, holy . . ." Rev. 4:8.

"You shall know the truth . . ." John 8:32.

"Lift up your heads . . ." Psa. 24:9.

"Lo, I am with you always . . ." Matt. 28:20.

39 "In Him we live and move . . ." Book of Common Prayer (1928) p. 587.

40 We are grateful to Rabbi Mel Gottlieb for permission to quote from his article "The Musar Community" which appeared in *Musar Anthology,* copyright © 1972 by Hillel Goldberg. This selection was reprinted with the permission of the author.

42 We would like to express our thanks to Abdullah Schleifer for giving us the information on Dhikers. For further reference see *The Transcendent Unity of Religions,* F. Schuon, (New York: Harper Torchback), pp. 134–138 and *The Mystics of Islam,* R. A. Nicholson, (Routledge & Kegan, 1970, reprint of a 1914 ed.)

III

MEANING BEYOND MEANINGS

45 "Be still and know that . . ." Psa. 46:10.

511 From Martin Luther's *How Man Should Pray, for Meister Peter, The Barber.* Written in 1534.

Page

52 E. Herman, *Creative Prayer,* (New York: Harper & Bros.), p. 79.

Louis Bouyer, *History of Christian Spirituality,* Vol. II, (New York: The Seabury Press, 1977), pp. 577–578.

53 J. M. Dechanet, *Christian Yoga,* (Burnes & Oates, 1960.)

54 The quotation from Lucius may be found in John Cassian's *Institutes.* Cassian was born in 360 and died in 435.

55 "Freely you have . . ." Matt. 10:8.

56 "Serve the Lord . . ." Psa. 100:2.

"Surely the Lord is . . ." Gen. 28:16.

The quotation from the anonymous woman comes from *Daily Strength for Daily Needs,* sel. by Mary Wilder Tileston, (Little Brown & Company, 1884.)

57 "Take my yoke upon you . . ." Matt. 11:29.

58 "Consecrate yourself today . . ." Ex. 32:29.

"The Lord your God . . ." Josh. 1:9 (RSV).

"Be strong and of . . ." Josh. 1:9 (RSV).

"Set a watch, O Lord . . ." Psa. 141:3.

"Judge not . . ." Matt. 7:1; Luke 6:37.

"Love your enemies . . ." Matt. 5:44.

"Be not overcome of evil . . ." Rom. 12:21.

"Truly this is a grief . . ." Jer. 10:19.

"Let not your heart . . ." John 14:27.

"When I sit in darkness . . ." Mic. 7:8.

"Therefore endure hardness . . ." II Tim. 2:3.

"Acquaint now thyself . . ." Job 22:21.

59 "Perfect love . . ." I John 4:18.

IV

FROM ANCIENT ROOTS

64 The Sunday Telegram (London) July 11, 1971, New Defenders of the Old Mass by Douglas Brown.

Louis Duchesne, *Christian Worship,* (London: SPCK, 1903.)

68 "Lift up your hearts . . ." This translation is used by several denominations today.

Cyprian. *The Oxford Dictionary of The Christian Church,* (London: The Oxford University Press, 1957), p. 1307.

Hippolytus. Bard Thompson, *Liturgies of the Western Church,* (New York: World Publishing, 1961), p. 20.

Jewish Benediction. Massey Hamilton Shepherd, Jr., *The Oxford American Prayer Book Commentary,* (New York: Oxford University Press, 1950), pp. 76–77.

"The Lord be with you . . ." this translation is used by several denominations today.

"common use among the Jews . . ." Shepherd, *op. cit.,* p. 70.

The Book of Ruth 2:4.

71 Greek Orthodox Liturgy. *The Divine Liturgy of St. John The Chryostom,* pp. 24–26.

72 The Sanctus (Holy, Holy, Holy) was incorporated into Christian services very early. The first section comes from Isaiah 6:1–3 and a form of it was used in Jewish worship. The second section comes from Matt. 21:9 where the crowds call out at Christ's entry into Jerusalem, Shepherd, *op. cit.,* pp. 76–77. The form of The Sanctus quoted

72 combines versions used in several liturgies today.

75 From *The Worshipbook—Services and Hymns.* Copyright © MCMLXXII, The Westminster Press. Used by permission. pp. 128–129, Litany for the Nation, portions of Form C.

V

MUSIC AND MEDITATION

82 "to a large extent . . ." Theodore M. Finney, *A History of Music,* (New York: Harcourt, Brace and Company, 1935), p. 31.

"Be filled with the Spirit . . ." 1 Cor. 14:15.

83 "semblance of musical unity . . ." Finney, *op. cit.,* p. 29.

84 Will Durant, *The Story of Civilization,* Vol. IV, (New York: Simon & Schuster, 1950), p. 895.

"Hymns in Greek and Latin . . ." Shepherd, *op. cit.,* p. 84 and *The Oxford Dictionary of The Christian Church, op. cit.,* p. 563.

85 "Glory be to God . . ." (Gloria in Excelsis). Combines versions used in several liturgies.

86 Louis Bouyer, *A History of Christian Spirituality,* Vol. III, (New York: The Seabury Press, 1977), p. 71. Albert Edward Bailey, *The Gospel in Hymns,* (New York: Charles Scribners' Sons, 1950), p. 309.

87 "stoned, mauled and ducked . . ." Bailey, *Ibid.,* p. 83.

88 Bailey, *Ibid.,* p. 85.

89 Bailey, *Ibid.,* p. 86.

90 "form so common to African songs . . ." James Weldon Johnson and J. Rosamond Johnson, *The Book of American Negro Spirituals,* (New York: The Viking Press, 1956), pp. 25–26.

93 Howard W. Odom and Guy B. Johnson, *Negro Workaday Songs,* (University of North Carolina Press, 1926.)

Gilbert Chase, *Americas Music,* rev. 2nd ed., (McGraw-Hill, 1955), p. 236.

94 "Geneva jiggs," "singing in her reign . . ." Bailey, *op. cit.,* p. 13.

95 "O sing unto the Lord . . ." Psa. 98:1.

98 "Wind blows where it wills . . ." John 3:8.

"The Lord of the Dance" by Sydney Carter. Used by permission of Galaxy Music Corporation.

VI

KNOWN BY HEART

103 "mosaic of allusion . . ." Shepherd, *op. cit.,* p. 26.

104 Karl Barth, *Prayer,* (The Westminster Press, 1952.)

105 Avery Brooke, *How to Meditate Without Leaving the World,* (Vineyard Books, 1975), p. 86.

106 "You are the salt . . ." Matt. 5:13.

"There was no room . . ." Luke 2:7.

"For where your treasure . . ." Luke 12:34.

"Faith is the substance . . ." Heb. 11:1.

"Be ye doers of the word . . ." Jas. 1:22.

"Follow me. I will make you . . ." Matt. 4:19.

Page

106 "What doth the Lord require . . ." Mic. 6:8.

"For he shall give his angels . . ." Psa. 91:11.

"You are the temple of God . . ." I Cor. 3:16.

"Be not conformed to this world . . ." Rom. 12:2.

"Take up your cross . . ." Matt. 16:24; Mark 8:34.

108 Rosary. John E. Sullivan, *Externals of The Catholic Church,* (P. J. Kennedy & Sons, 1917); Catherine Frederic, *Handbook of Catholic Practices,* (Christian Classics, Inc., 1963); Eithne Wilkins, *The Rose Garden Game,* (Gollancz, 1969.)

"Forgive what we have been . . ." *Services for Trial Use,* (New York: Church Hymnal Corp. © Copyright 1971 by Charles Mortimer Guilbert as custodian of the Standard Book of Common Prayer.), p. 69.

"May Christ dwell in our hearts . . ." Eph. 3:17–18.

109 "The Lord is with thee . . ." Luke 1:28.

111 Michel Quoist, *Prayers,* (Sheed & Ward, 1963.)

111 "I said to the man at the gate . . ." from *God Knows* written by Minnie Louise Haskin in 1908. This was quoted by King George VI of England in a radio broadcast, December 25, 1939. At that time the authorship was uknown.

112 John Calvin, *Commentary on The Psalms* written in 1563.

Thomas Merton, *Bread in the Wilderness.* Copyright 1953 by Our Lady of Gethsemani Monastery. Reprinted by permission of New Directions Publishing Corp., p. 3.

113 Mary Ellen Chase, *Psalms for the Common Reader,* (New York: W. W. Norton, 1962), p. 25.

EPILOGUE

132 "Incline your ear . . ." Isa. 55:3.

134 Martha and Mary. Luke 10:38–42.

"Christ has died . . ." This version of an ancient Easter greeting appears in Roman Catholic annd Episcopal liturgies.

135 "They that wait . . ." Isa. 40:31.

HIDDEN IN PLAIN SIGHT

was set in
Times Roman with Palatino display

Designed by
Laurel Casazza and M. B. Glick.